AT THE ALTAR OF

SEXUAL IDOLATRY

WORKBOOK

STEVE GALLAGHER

AT THE ALTAR OF
SEXUAL
IDOLATRY
WORKBOOK

"Purity for Life"

www.purelifeministries.org

888.PURELIFE

Also available by Steve Gallagher:

At The Altar Of Sexual Idolatry
A Biblical Guide to Counseling the Sexual Addict
Fron Ashes to Beauty
He Leads Me Beside Still Waters
How America Lost Her Innocence
Intoxicated With Babylon
Irresistible to God
A Lamp Unto My Feet
Living in Victory
Out of the Depths of Sexual Sin
Pressing on Toward the Heavenly Calling
Standing Firm Through the Great Apostasy
The Walk of Repentance

For these books and other teaching materials please contact:

Pure Life Ministries

14 School Street
Dry Ridge, KY 41035
(888) PURELIFE - to order
(859) 824-4444
(859) 813-0005 FAX
www.purelifeministries.org

EAN 978-0-9702202-1-9

CONTENTS:

PART 4: The Way Out

INTRODUCTION:

The purpose of this workbook is to help the reader of *At the Altar of Sexual Idolatry* to focus on the major themes presented in each chapter. In doing so, the reader can expect to gain a better understanding of the issues and truths discussed throughout the book. While reading alone is helpful, having to search for the answers to questions and then write them down will enhance one's retention of the important steps provided for overcoming sexual sin.

With that in mind, several questions have been generated from each of the seventeen chapters. You will find that I often quoted sentences which contain the answer to a particular question. The questions are also arranged in accordance with the order in which the chapters were written. For instance, the answer to question number 7 will always be located in the chapter somewhere between the answers to questions 6 and 8.

Finding the answers will not always be easy. You may have to go back and forth over portions of the text. That's the way it is supposed to be! The more you have to search for answers, the more likely the material of the book is going to "get into you." If you should come across a question that you just cannot find the answer to, skip it until you have completed the entire workbook.

Then, *only as a last resort,* you can look up the answer in the back of the book. If you look it up while you are still in the chapter, you will not be able to find that answer without seeing the other answers for that chapter. This would only serve to defeat the whole purpose of this exercise.

The answers to the scriptural questions are not provided. There are two reasons for this. First, people use different translations of the Bible, which will affect the way the answer reads. Secondly, most of the answers will be based upon the reader's own perspective. Please keep in mind that I use the New American Standard version of the Bible and some of the questions reflect the wording of that translation.

You will experience a wide range of feelings as you read *At the Altar of Sexual Idolatry.* Sometimes it will be painful, while other times will be filled with hope as you sense God's loving presence there to help you. Make notes as you go through this. One day it will be a real blessing to look back at the different spiritual and emotional experiences you have during this special time in your life.

I hope this workbook is a blessing to you as you seek the biblical answers for your needs.

Steve Gallagher, Author

CHAPTER ONE:

SEXUAL IDOLATRY

Study Questions

1. Name the eight examples of things "people prostrate themselves before."

   a. Career   b.   c.

   d. homes   e.   f.

   g.   h.

2. Name the seven different sexual addiction "routines" listed.

   a.   b.   c.

   d.   e.   f.

   g.

3. Which of these routines "closely resembles that of the exhibitionist?"

4. Complete the sentence which begins, "Their actual routines may differ…"

5. What are the two basic disciplines "the typical 'sexual addict' can maintain?"

    a.

    b.

6. Complete the sentence which begins, "Loved ones usually feel…"

7. What would it mean for the sexual addict, "To accept responsibility for his life and his own failures?"

8. Complete the sentence which begins, "This blameshifting process..."

9. What does the sexual addict do when "he knows that what he is doing is wrong?"

10. Who is it who "will often be overly sensitive to criticism?"

11. Complete the sentence which begins, "Another phenomenon the sexual..."

12. What does "Sexual addiction/bondage" transcend?

What the Scriptures Say

1. Read the following verses and write down what you learn about sin:

   Proverbs 5:22

   Proverbs 7:22-23

   Proverbs 26:11

2. Read II Peter 2:9-22 and answer the following questions.

   In verse 9, Peter describes the "godly" and the "unrighteous." In the rest of the chapter, he lists a number of characteristics of the unrighteous. Write down ten of these characteristics.

   a.   b.

   c.   d.

e.   f.

g.   h.

i.   j.

3. Write out II Peter 2:18-19.

4. Explain what you think Peter is saying in verse 21.

Personal Examination

1. What did you learn about sexual addiction from this chapter?

2. What did you learn about yourself from this chapter?

Group Discussion Questions

1. Without being too specific, how did your problems with sexual sin begin?
2. Could you relate to the "vicious cycle of self-destruction and degradation" the author discusses?
3. Did you have a difficult time accepting responsibility for your actions?
4. How did sin bring out the worst in you?
5. Did you ever feel as though you were the only one with your problem?

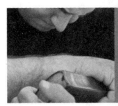

CHAPTER TWO:

DEVELOPING CONVICTIONS ABOUT LUST AND MASTURBATION

Study Questions

1. What will "the one who is looking for the path of least resistance in life" lack?

2. What will this man do "when convicted over his sinful thoughts and actions?"

3. Complete the sentence which begins, "Just as the physical heart pumps life-giving blood…"

4. Write out the three definitions provided for the Greek word *epithumeo.*

    a.

    b.

    c.

5. Describe the "two primary categories" of lust.

    a.   *reactive:*

    b.   *proactive:*

6. List five characteristics of the "dream girls" in a "man's world of imagination."

    a.

    b.

    c.

    d.

    e.

7. What did Jesus face when He "began His ministry in Israel?"

8. Complete the sentence which begins, "He said exactly what He meant…"

9. Complete the sentence which begins, "For instance, if we are talking about…"

10. When would the word stumble "not be the appropriate term to use?"

11. Complete the sentence which begins, "While occasions do exist wherein believers remain needlessly old-fashioned regarding particular issues…"

12. Who views "sex as simply one room in the vast pleasure palace of life?"

What The Scriptures Say

1. Write out five of the verses about the human heart listed on pages 38-39.

    a.

    b.

    c.

    d.

    e.

2. Read the following verses and explain in your own words what you learn about lust.

    Proverbs 6:25

Job 31:1

Matthew 5:27-28

II Peter 2:14a

3. Proverbs 7 describes how a harlot seduces a young man walking down the street. Rewrite a condensed version of this chapter in your own words substituting Internet pornography for the harlot. How would it approach you? How would it seduce you? What could the consequences be?

Personal Examination

1. What did you learn about lust from this chapter?

2. What did you learn about masturbation from this chapter?

3. Do you feel more convicted about the sinfulness of lust
    and masturbation than you did before reading this chapter?

Group Discussion Questions:

1. Has this chapter altered your perspectives on the sinfulness
    of lust? If so, how?
2. Has this chapter altered your perspectives on the sinfulness
    of masturbation? If so, how?
3. What insights have you gained on the make-up of the
    human heart?
4. How do you feel the world's attitudes regarding sexuality
    have influenced the Church's overall mindset regarding
    this subject?
5. Discuss how the average believer today would differ in his
    viewpoints about pornography and sexual sin compared to
    the typical Christian of a century ago.

CHAPTER THREE:

THE SPIRAL OF DEGRADATION

Study Questions

1. Write out the three parts of "the old adage":

   a.

   b.

   c.

2. List the seven steps down into *The Spiral of Degradation*.

   a.

   b.

   c.

   d.

   e.

f.

g.

3. What is the "attitude which sneaks in very subtly?"

4. Complete the sentence which begins, "Once a person reaches this point…"

5. List the three things that happen to a man every time he "looks at pornography or gives over to some other form of sexual sin."

    a.

    b.

    c.

6. What three statements are listed which "are typical of what the deceived person tells himself?"

    a.

    b.

    c.

7. What did the early church fathers consider to be the "worst aspect of hell?"

8. What have I had "men confess to me?"

9. What is "one of the terrifying realities about this Being, Jehovah?"

10. What happens when "that protective grace is eventually withdrawn?"

11. What are the four things which keep the sexual addict "in check?"

    a.

    b.

    c.

    d.

What the Scriptures Say

1. Read Romans 6:12-16 and answer the following questions.

    Write out verses 12-15, replacing the word "sin" with "sexual sin" (or "commit sexual sin").

    Considering your past struggles, what does verse 16 mean to you?

2. Read Ephesians 4:17-19 and answer the following questions.

    Paul instructs the reader, "…walk no longer just as the Gentiles also walk…" and then gives eight characteristics of what this means. List those characteristics.

    a.

    b.

    c.

d.

e.

f.

g.

h.

Paul said that the Gentiles were "excluded from the life of God." Explain what you think happens to the man who allows his mind to become darkened and his heart to become hardened and calloused?

Personal Examination

1. What did you learn about "The Spiral of Degradation?"

2. What did you learn about yourself in this chapter?

Group Discussion Questions

1. Discuss how "the old adage" that opens the chapter has been true in your life.
2. Can you look back and see how you had an ungrateful spirit at one time?
3. If so, how has that changed in your life?
4. Did you ever deceive yourself about your sin with any of the statements the author lists? (see pp. 54-55)
5. Did sin become increasingly less fulfilling for you?

CHAPTER FOUR:

THE NEED TO
LIVE IN THE LIGHT

Study Questions

1. What did the stories in the beginning of the chapter "represent?"

2. What are the three reasons given which help to motivate men to "keep their sin hidden?"

    a.

    b.

    c.

3. In your own words, describe the term "inside world."

4. What is said about "the deepest part of his inner man?"

5. In what ways have you been "outward" around other Christians?

6. Complete the three following statements or phrases about the progression of fear.

   a. I suppose it begins…

b. The fear is deepened...

c. and becomes embedded...

7. Complete the sentence which begins, "In essence, they ignore..."

8. What is a man saying, in essence, when he "blameshifts, minimizes or conceals his sin?"

9. What will the man eventually discover "who thinks he can continue hiding his sin?"

10. In your own words, explain the "correlation between a person's involvement with sin and his awareness of it."

11. Complete the sentence which begins, "Keeping himself hyped..."

12. How would you respond to men who say they "could not bear to hurt their wives who are unaware" of their sexual sin?

13. Read the final section of this chapter and describe in your own words the difference between accountability and discipleship.

What the Scriptures Say

1. Read Luke 12:1-5 and answer the following questions.

   What are the three things which Jesus commands us to do in this passage of Scripture?

   a.

   b.

   c.

   Describe what hypocrisy has to do with things which are "covered up" and "hidden," and words spoken "in the dark" and "whispered in the inner rooms."

   Read this passage of Scripture over again carefully. In your own words, what would you say that Jesus is saying to the reader?

Personal Examination

1. What did you learn about living in the light from this chapter?

2. What did you learn about yourself from this chapter?

Group Discussion Questions

1. Could you relate to any of the three stories at the beginning of the chapter?
2. Have you ever kept sin hidden?
3. Have you attempted to make yourself look as though you were doing better than you really were spiritually?
4. Can you see how sin deceives the heart?
5. Have you humbled yourself to be discipled by someone more mature than you are?

CHAPTER FIVE:

THE PROCESS OF SIN

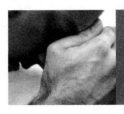

Study Questions

1. According to the Pulpit Commentary, what is "the impelling power which seduces towards evil?"

2. According to the Pulpit Commentary, what are the five things that sin kills?

   a.   b.

   c.   d.

   e.

3. Write out the quote of Thomas à Kempis.

4. What does "honey" represent?

5. What does "smooth oil" represent?

6. Give Jenson's definition of "a trigger."

7. What are the "three circumstances that usually" prove disastrous?

    a.

    b.

    c.

8. Can you see how these three circumstances have affected your ability to withstand temptation? Explain your answer.

9. Why are "these thoughts…difficult to control?"

10. According to Dietrich Bonhœffer, what does Satan fill us with?

11. In your own words describe how people fool themselves when "moving toward sin."

12. What takes over "once the body is in motion?"

13. From your own experience, why is the actual act of sin so often a disappointment?

14. Write out three resolutions that you have made in the past.

    a.

    b.

    c.

15. How can you prepare now to face future temptations in your specific area of struggle?

16. Complete the sentence which begins, "I had become so…"

What the Scriptures Say

1. Read James 1:13-16 and answer the following questions.

   Why do you think some people might say, "I am being tempted by God?"

   In light of your own experience, what do you think that James meant when he said that a man who is tempted "is carried away and enticed by his own lust?"

2. Read Proverbs 5:3-13 and answer the following questions.

    What is Solomon's main piece of advice in this section of scripture?

    What are the five things that will happen if you do not heed this advice?

    a.

    b.

    c.

    d.

    e.

Personal Examination

1. What did you learn about the process of sin from this chapter?

2. What did you learn about your own sin from this chapter?

Group Discussion Questions

1. How have you responded to temptation in the past?
2. How have "the three circumstances" affected your ability to withstand temptation? (see p. 83)
3. Have you ever insisted on keeping a job which "made provision for the flesh?"
4. What is the difference between a resolution and repentance?
5. Discuss the truth of I Corinthians 10:13.

CHAPTER SIX:

THE ROOT ISSUES

Study Questions

1. In your own words, briefly describe what Sigmund Freud taught was the key to helping a counselee "cope with the daily stresses of life."

2. What does the Bible teach "the Christian who is struggling with sinful habits to deal with?"

3. Complete the sentence which begins, "The truth is, before…"

4. What is "the first step toward victory?"

5. Write out "one of the 'cop-outs' I have heard many times."

6. What does "habitual sexual sin" stem from?

7. According to Romans 8:29, what is God's great purpose in the life of a believer?

8. What "way of life" must the sexual addict embrace to find victory over sin?

9. According to the author, what is pride?

10. List the seven different variations of pride.

   a.

   b.

   c.

   d.

   e.

   f.

   g.

What the Scriptures Say

1. Read the following verses and write down what you learn about pride and humility.

Psalm 101:5

Psalm 138:6

James 4:10

Romans 12:3

Romans 12:16

Luke 22:26

2. Consider what you have learned about the different kinds of pride and what you have learned in the Bible about the importance of humility. Pick out three types of pride that you struggle with and describe how they affect those around you. Also tell why you feel it is important to allow God to work them out of your life.

a.

b.

c.

3. Read Luke 9:22-25 and answer the following questions.

   According to verse 22, what did the King of kings have to look forward to?

   According to verse 23, what are the three things His followers should do?

   a.

   b.

   c.

   According to verses 24 & 25, what will happen to the man who attempts to "save his life?"

Personal Examination

1. What did you learn about the roots of sexual addiction from this chapter?

2. What did you learn about yourself from this chapter?

Group Discussion Questions

1. Have you ever had the attitude that you have your problems because of what someone else did or did not do to you?
2. Discuss why the doctrine of the depravity of man is so important to cling to in this day and age.
3. Read and discuss Luke 9:22-25.
4. Can you relate to any of the different types of pride?
5. Why is it important for God to humble us?

CHAPTER SEVEN:

FREEDOM COMES SLOWLY
FOR A REASON

Study Questions

1. In what two ways does God transform a man?

   a.

   b.

2. How does the Lord usually deal "with those in sexual sin?"

3. Complete the sentence which begins, "One of the things…"

4. In your own words, how would you say that God uses a man's sin to "eventually draw him closer to Himself?"

5. Complete the sentence which begins, "God is often more…"

6. In the section called "God's Timing," the man who has been "set free from his sin" is asked four questions. Write out these questions, but instead of writing the word "his," personalize each question. I will give the first one as an example.

   a. Will my selfishness simply be spent on being a workaholic?

   b.

   c.

   d.

7. What life "is not spared the experience of pain?"

8. Give the five "synonyms for the word conquer."

    a.   b.

    c.   d.

    e.

9. In O.T. times, the Lord required the Israelites to war against
    the idolatrous nations around them. Explain in your own
    words why the Lord would want you to learn to battle
    against your own flesh.

10. Write out (and answer for yourself) the four questions
    regarding "how long it will take" to receive victory over sin.

    a.

    b.

c.

d.

11. Does habitual sin seem like a mountain for you to overcome? Do you see how using the biblical steps outlined in this book could help you conquer that mountain? Write out a statement of determination, that with God's help, you will overcome.

What the Scriptures Say

1. Read II Corinthians 4:16-18 and answer the following questions.

    The Apostle Paul suffered greatly during his years of ministry. Considering these verses, why do you think he had so much joy in life?

What would you say is the importance of your inner man "being renewed day by day?"

Considering verse 18, what was Paul fixing his attention on?

Write out Colossians 3:1-2

Personal Examination

1. What did you learn about why it takes time to come into freedom?

2. What did you learn about what you can expect for yourself after reading this chapter?

Group Discussion Questions

1. Spend your time discussing the reasons why freedom comes slowly:
    a. If we were freed instantly, we might not appreciate our freedom.
    b. The process teaches us to rely upon God.
    c. God is very concerned that we mature as Christians also during this period of restoration.
    d. God wants us to learn to battle the desires of the flesh.

CHAPTER EIGHT:

HOW MUCH DO
YOU CARE?

Study Questions

1. Explain what advantage there is to seeing the life of someone who has overcome habitual sin.

2. According to Frank Worthen, when do "we accept the conclusion that we can't change ourselves?"

3. What benefits does Worthen list to keeping sin?

   a.

   b.

   c.

4. What conclusion does he suggest to the one who is not changing?

5. How would you relate the boxer illustration to your need to change?

6. In your own words, explain the "If-Then Principle."

7. What "was established by God as the means to receiving His help?"

8. How would you compare your situation to the history of "the nation of Israel?"

9. Who is "the center of the Christian faith?"

10. What is our faith "inextricably tied to?"

11. Write out the definition of believe the *Vine's Expository Dictionary* gives.

12. What is "one of the terrible and frightening aspects of sin?"

13. Take a few minutes to write out your own "believing prayer."

What the Scriptures Say

1. I once did a Bible study that greatly affected my life. The conviction had been growing within me that "our faith is inextricably tied to who He is." Everything in our lives hinges on our trust in God. With this in mind, I would like you to look up the following verses and, just to get a fuller picture of this, replace the word faith with the phrase, "the knowledge of the good and merciful character of God." I'll do the first one as an example.

   Matthew 6:30 "But if God so arrays the grass of the field, which is alive today and tomorrow is thrown into the furnace, will He not much more do so for you, O men of little *knowledge of the good and merciful character of God?*"

   Habakkuk 2:4

   Matthew 9:22

Romans 10:17

II Corinthians 5:7

I Timothy 6:10

James 1:3

James 1:6

I Peter 1:7

I John 5:4

Personal Examination

1. What did you learn about having a sincere desire for victory from this chapter?

2. What did you learn about your own level of determination from this chapter?

Group Discussion Questions

1. Read and discuss Luke 11:5-8 in light of desiring victory over sin.
2. Read and discuss Luke 18:1-7 in light of desiring victory over sin.
3. Do you ever struggle with wanting to overcome badly enough to do what it takes to get that victory?
4. Discuss faith in the context of one's intimate, personal relationship with God.
5. How does your trust in Him affect your cry for help?

CHAPTER NINE:

THE SINFUL FLESH

Study Questions

1. What are "the three forces which work tirelessly to compel us toward sin?"

   a.   b.   c.

2. What is it that "God wants?"

3. Complete the sentence which begins, "An alcoholic could go..."

4. What are the three things the flesh "is only interested in?"

    a.   b.

    c.

5. What is "every human being" born with?

6. What words are used by the Bible to describe the inner man?

7. How does "the wide variety of outside stimuli" enter a person's mind?

8. Complete the sentence which begins, "Just as the flesh grows..."

9. Practice is an important element in the process of changing our habits. Complete the following three sentences:

a. "If we practice (or sow) ungodliness…"

b. "By the same token, if we practice godliness…"

c. "Feelings always…"

10. According to Dr. Jay Adams, why do "Christians give up?"

11. According to Adams, how many total weeks "of proper daily effort" does it take "to make the practice part of oneself?"

12. What is "the primary enemy we will face?"

What the Scriptures Say

1. Read the sixth chapter of Romans and answer the following questions.

   In verse 7 Paul says: "for he who has died is freed from sin." There are two perspectives on this. Some think that it means that a believer can no longer be bound by sin. He simply must accept this "truth" by faith and the sin will go away. I agree with others that what Paul is saying is that the believer has been freed from the *legal authority* sin once had over him. He "has been bought with a price..." He is now a child of God and sin can have no dominion over him that he does not allow it to have. Whereas, before he came to the Lord he was completely subject to sin, now the power of God is available to him to free him from habitual sin. Carefully examine Romans chapters six, seven and eight. Do you see anything in these chapters which expresses the idea that a person becomes freed from sin by "believing" he is free?

What are the commands given in 6:12-13?

2. Read Romans 8:5-8 and describe in your own words what Paul is teaching.

3. In I Corinthians 2:16 Paul makes the statement, "But we have the mind of Christ." Again, these same teachers say that the

Apostle was making a blanket statement of fact and the mind of Christ will be ours as we "accept it by faith." I propose another perspective: Believers have *access* to the mind of Christ and can enter into His thinking, perspectives and compassion as they mature in the faith. Read the following verses and write down a simple "yes" or "no" to whether or not you believe the Corinthians had the mind of Christ.

I Corinthians 1:11-12

I Corinthians 3:1-4

Paul had the mind of Christ because he lived an extremely consecrated life. People can claim to have the mind of Christ, but the reality of it is proven through their love, humility, and godliness; not through presumptuous assertions.

4. Read Hebrews 11:6. Would you say that faith has more to do with a personal, daily trust in God or in the acceptance of doctrinal beliefs expressed by men?

5. There are over 1,000 commands given to the believer in the New Testament. Would you say that God is looking for us to live godly, consecrated lives?

Personal Examination

1. What did you learn about the importance of overcoming the desires of the flesh from this chapter?

2. What did you learn about your own nature from this chapter?

Group Discussion Questions

1. Read and discuss the struggles Paul expressed in Romans 7:15-25.
2. Can you relate to these battles within?
3. Discuss the physical buildup which occurs in a man after several days without sex.
4. Discuss how habits play such a prominent part in our daily lives.
5. How could one establish new habits?

CHAPTER TEN:

SEPARATING FROM THE WORLD

Study Questions

1. Complete the sentence which begins, "With such overwhelming…"

2. Write out the statement of Lester Sumrall.

3. What has "God called us to" do?

4. What does Dr. Jenson say to Christians who claim that television "does not affect" them?

5. Answer the following rhetorical questions asked in the book:

    "The believer who watches a fun-loving Budweiser commercial might not run right out and buy a six-pack of beer, but how does its message affect his need for inner sobriety?"

    "What is the cumulative effect of seeing sexy women night after night on TV?"

    "How is he affected when he accumulates countless hours watching situation comedies which mock everything which is decent?"

6. According to Don Wildmon, what is "the greatest educator we have?"

7. What image does Peter's exhortation to "be sober and vigilant" create in one's mind?

8. Complete the two following statements:

"Rather than aggressively tearing down the strongholds of the enemy and waging war for the souls of our loved ones…"

"Instead of affecting the world around us for the cause of Christ…"

What the Scriptures Say

1. Read Matthew 7:13. Would you say that those who are subjecting themselves to the spirit of this world are on the narrow path or the broad way?

2. Read II Corinthians 6:14-7:1 and answer the following questions.

    In verse 14, Paul uses three descriptive terms describing the relationship we should not have with unbelievers. In the NASB, they are "bound," "partnership," and "fellowship." What are they in your translation (if it is different)?

    What does God command of His people in verse 17?

    What three things does He promise in verses 17 and 18 to those who will do this?

    a.

    b.

    c.

Write out II Corinthians 7:1.

3. Read Romans 12:1-2 and answer the following questions.

    What does Paul command us to do in the first verse?

    In verse 2 he commands us not to "be conformed to this
    world." List three ways you feel that you are still conformed
    to this world.

    a.

    b.

    c.

Personal Examination

1. What did you learn about separating from the world from this chapter?

2. What did you learn about your own love for this world from this chapter?

Group Discussion Questions

1. What are some ways the spirit of this world can affect your life?
2. Read and discuss II Corinthians 6:14-7:1 and its ramifications for today's Christian.
3. Can you see how the enemy has used the same strategy on believers that the communists used in their bid to take over the world?
4. Discuss Wildmon's allegation that television is basically defaming Christians. (see p. 167)

CHAPTER ELEVEN:

BATTLES IN THE SPIRITUAL REALM

Study Questions

1. In your own words describe the teachings about spiritual warfare which are at the two "opposite end[s] of the spectrum."

    a.

    b.

2. Complete the following sentences or phrases:

    "To the one who struggles with depression…"

    "For those who battle a hot temper…"

"for an exaggerated sex drive..."

3. Give a brief explanation of the spiritual law in Galatians 6:7-8.

4. Give a brief explanation of the spiritual law in Matthew 23:12.

5. What is "the primary point of" John's statement?

6. According to Dr. Unger, what happens when a believer yields to "pressure, suggestion, and temptation?"

7. Would you say that the enemy or demons can attack believers in whatever way and to whatever degree they wish? Explain your answer.

8. Describe in your own words how a stronghold is created within a person.

9. Who is it who has a "vague concept" of victory?

10. Explain in your own words "the place of refuge for the believer."

What the Scriptures Say

1. Read Ephesians 6:10-18 and answer the following questions.

    According to verse 10, where does our strength come from?

    According to verse 11, why should we "put on the full armor of God?"

    What are the four enemies listed in verse 12?

    a.

    b.

    c.

    d.

    In verses 14-17 there are six articles of armor with corresponding spiritual disciplines aligned with each. List each spiritual discipline and describe in your own words how you feel that it would help you to "stand firm against the schemes of the devil."

a.

b.

c.

d.

e.

f.

2. Read John 14:30 and explain in your own words why this is or is not true of you.

Personal Examination

1. What did you learn about spiritual warfare from this chapter?

2. What did you learn about your own struggles with the enemy from this chapter?

Group Discussion Questions

1. Can you think of any temptation to fall into sin you have encountered in the past which you are fairly certain the enemy arranged?
2. Read II Corinthians 10:3-6 and discuss the implications of these verses.
3. Read the illustration about Joseph (using Job's story) and discuss what conversations might have occurred between the devil and God about you. (see pp. 180-181)
4. Have different men read the following verses: II Corinthians 2:11; 11:3; 11:14-15; I Peter 5:8. Discuss what you learn about the enemy from these verses.

CHAPTER TWELVE:

THE PLACE OF BROKENNESS AND REPENTANCE

Study Questions

1. Complete the sentence which begins, "The common philosophy…"

2. Describe in your own words the "solution" that "has been termed 'maintenance.'"

3. What is "the answer for believers?"

4. How does this change come about?

5. What must take place "in order for God to get a person to the place where he is able to forsake the idols of his life?"

6. Regarding the human will, what "is sheer nonsense?"

7. Complete the sentence which begins, "*Spiritual repentance is…*"

8. Explain in your own words the difference between Zacchaeus
    and the man who agreed to follow Jesus but first wanted to
    say good-bye to those at home.

9. What is it that "repentance describes?"

10. In your own words, describe what part being "poor in
    spirit" plays in the process of the repentance of sin.

11. In your own words, describe what part "mourning" plays
    in the process of the repentance of sin.

12. In your own words, describe what part "meekness" plays in the process of the repentance of sin.

What the Scriptures Say

1. Read the following verses and write down what you learn about God's will:

Matthew 7:21

Matthew 12:50

Matthew 26:42

John 7:17

Ephesians 6:6

I Thessalonians 4:3-5

Personal Examination

1. What did you learn about repentance from this chapter?

2. What did you learn about your own will from this chapter?

Group Discussion Questions

1. Have different men read a beautitude and discuss its place in
   the process of repentance:
   vs. 3   Blessed are the poor in spirit, for theirs is the
   kingdom of heaven.
   vs. 4   Blessed are those who mourn, for they shall
   be comforted.
   vs. 5   Blessed are the gentle, for they shall inherit the earth.
   vs. 6   Blessed are those who hunger and thirst for righ-
   teousness, for they shall be satisfied.
   vs. 7   Blessed are the merciful, for they shall receive mercy.
   vs. 8   Blessed are the pure in heart, for they shall see God.
   vs. 9   Blessed are the peacemakers, for they shall be called
   sons of God.

CHAPTER THIRTEEN:

DISCIPLINED FOR HOLINESS

Study Questions

1. What does the Bible use "the term fool to describe?"

2. Read the letter to Lucy and explain in your own words how it is that someone can seem to be receiving the "blessings of God" and yet not even be saved.

3. Explain how the illustration about the man with the broken arm who would not go to the doctor relates to your own life (if it does).

4. What can one "readily distinguish" from "these passages?"

5. When Jesus rebuked Peter, what was "His only concern?"

6. Complete the sentence which begins, "Sometimes a sharp..."

7. If you were "to spend some time reading the epistles of First and Second Peter," what would you "read?"

8. What is "the problem with this sort of thinking?"

9. What "thinking is sheer fantasy?"

10. What are "the words of a friend?"

11. How does holiness come?

What the Scriptures Say

1. Write out in your own words what you learn about fools from the following verses:

   Proverbs 1:7

   Proverbs 1:22

   Proverbs 14:16

   Proverbs 17:10

   Proverbs 18:2

   Proverbs 23:9

   Ecclesiastes 7:4

2. Read Proverbs 5:7-13 and describe how this relates to your own life.

3. Read the following verses and explain in your own words what you learn about biblical discipline.

Proverbs 12:1

Proverbs 13:1

Proverbs 13:18

Proverbs 15:5

Proverbs 15:31

Proverbs 15:32

Personal Examination

1. What did you learn about God's process of discipline from this chapter?

2. What did you learn about your own reactions to His discipline from this chapter?

Group Discussion Questions

1. Discuss the "lifestyle of instant gratification, selfish indulgence, superficial relationships, and shallow commitments" we have been bombarded with and how it has encouraged sexual sin.
2. Can you see how the Lord was helping Peter through all the rebukes he received?
3. What do you suppose would have happened with Peter's life if he would have refused the correction God brought into his life?
4. Can you see how foolish it would be to go through life continually looking for a quick and painless solution to a problem that is rooted in one's character?

CHAPTER FOURTEEN:

WALKING IN THE SPIRIT

Study Questions

1. What must the man do "if he wants to overcome habitual sin?"

2. Complete both halves of Paul's conditional promise.

   IF...

   THEN...

3. Who was it "who first used the term *walk?*"

4.   What would be the "modern day" term for *walk*?

5.   "When Paul says to 'walk in the Spirit,' he is describing" what?

6.   Read the section entitled, "The Daily Sustenance of Prayer" and, using the elements provided, write out a plan of action for establishing a prayer life.

What will be your "style" of prayer?

Where will you pray?

When will you pray?

How long will you pray each day?

How can you make worship a part of your prayer time?

7. Complete the sentence which begins, "One problem sexual addicts…"

8. What must there be "before the Word can be implanted?"

9. What "goes forth as the Scripture is approached *in the right spirit?*"

10. According to Dr. Jenson, what does it mean "to become 'transformed by the renewing of your mind?'"

11. According to Jay Adams, what is "the counselor's biblical answer?"

What the Scriptures Say

1. Read and pray over Galatians 5:19-21. Pick out three of these characteristics which apply to your life and describe your struggle with each.

   a.

   b.

   c.

2. Read James 1:21-25 and answer the following questions.

   What are the two things which you must put aside/lay apart/- get rid of before the word will be implanted?

   a.

   b.

Write out verse 22.

What would you say it means to be a "doer of the word?"

According to verses 23 and 24, what happens to the person who "is a hearer of the word and not a doer?"

What does the person do who "shall be blessed in what he does?"

3. Read the following verses and tell in your own words what the word will do for the person who heeds it.

   Proverbs 2:10

   Proverbs 2:12

   Proverbs 6:23-24

   Proverbs 7:5

Personal Examination

1. What did you learn about walking in the Spirit from this chapter?

2. What did you learn about your own walk with God from this chapter?

Group Discussion Questions

1. What does it really mean to walk in the Spirit?
2. Read and discuss John 15:1-5.
3. What kind of problems do you have maintaining your devotional life?
4. How will a devotional life affect the person who struggles with habitual sin?
5. How will it help a struggling believer to really begin to live out the Word of God?

CHAPTER FIFTEEN:

OVERCOMING LUST

Study Questions

1. What is required "if the mind becomes corrupted with lust?"

2. What does "the spirit of this world" create?

3. Complete the sentence which begins, "In practical terms…"

4. Complete the following sentences:

    a. "…a mall…promotes…"

    b. "…a boxing match…incites…"

    c. "…a bar, the ambience puts him in a…"

5. What must the person do "who is going to get the victory over lust?"

6. What is "hellish living?"

7. How does one "climb right out of that pit?"

8. What is "the message behind lust?"

9. What is "the feeling lodged within the grateful heart?"

10. Which of the boys could you relate more to--Johnny or Juan? Explain your answer.

11. What is it "that must be encouraged and nurtured?"

12. Briefly explain in your own words the "two basic things one can do" to develop a grateful spirit.

    a.

    b.

13. What must happen to a man "if he is going to be cleansed on the inside?"

14. Define love, "in simplest terms."

15. Having read the rest of the chapter, write down some ideas you might have about how you can get involved in helping others.

What the Scriptures Say

1. Read the following verses and write down what it is that
    God gives the believer.

    Romans 6:23

    II Peter 1:3

    Matthew 16:19

    Luke 10:19

2. Read Luke 11:37-44 and answer the following questions.

    According to verse 39 and what you know about the
    Pharisees, would you say that their outward lives were in
    order? Explain your answer.

    According to verse 40, would you say that Jesus thinks that
    what goes on inside a person is just as important as what
    they do outwardly? Explain your answer.

    According to verse 43, what did the Pharisees love?

Can you see how the Pharisees had learned to do all of the outward things to appear as though they were godly, but in reality they had little love for God or others? What does this story teach you about your own walk with God?

Personal Examination

1. What did you learn about overcoming lust from this chapter?

2. What did you learn about your own struggles from this chapter?

Group Discussion Questions

1. What are some ways the spirit of this world can create an atmosphere conducive to sexual lust right in the home?
2. What can one do to maintain a spiritually clean environment at home?
3. As a group, come up with a list of thirty things you appreciate about your pastor (even if different churches are represented).
4. Can you see how selfishness can keep a person locked in sin?
5. As a group, make up a list of things that the men of the congregation could do around the church to be a blessing to the pastor and to others.

CHAPTER SIXTEEN:

HOW TO BE A GREAT LOVER
(A WORD TO MARRIED MEN)

Study Questions

1. What does "the world's presentation of a great lover" mask?

2. What is "the world's concept of love?"

3. What can one "safely say" about the world's concept of commitment?

4. Complete the sentence which begins, "This level of devotion…"

5. What is "the foundation of biblical love" based upon?

6. Complete the sentence which begins, "The man who wishes…"

7. What will happen "as the husband learns to treat his wife with tenderness?"

8. What will happen "if the husband can restore the trust that he has shattered?"

9. Write out the statement of C.S. Lewis.

10. What is "the enviable position" some men are in?

11. What do "men keep themselves in bondage to?"

12. Complete the sentence which begins, "*If a man will learn...*"

13. What is "part of the problem with sexual addicts?"

14. What is "the problem with trying to live life at 80 m.p.h.?"

15. Read the story at the end of the chapter and relate it to your love for your wife.

What the Scriptures Say

1. Read Luke 6:27-38 and answer the following questions.

According to verses 27 and 28, what are the three practical things a believer can do to love his enemies?

a.

b.

c.

Write out I Peter 3:9.

According to verse 31, how should you be treating your wife?

Explain what you think Jesus is saying in verse 32.

According to verse 35, what is required of us in order to receive a great reward and "be sons of the Most High?"

Many people quote verse 38 as a formula to getting God to give them money. But considering the context of what Jesus was talking about, explain what you think He was referring to.

2.　Read I Corinthians 13:4-8. Pick out four of the "love principles" and explain how you will improve the way you treat your wife in these areas.

a.

b.

c.

d.

Personal Examination

1. What did you learn about the importance of loving your wife from this chapter?

2. What did you learn about the way you treat your wife from this chapter?

Group Discussion Questions

1. Why is it important to treat your wife with love?
2. Read and discuss I Corinthians 13:4-8 in relation to the marriage bed. (Be discreet.)
3. Read and discuss the story in Numbers 11:4-6 in relation to being exhilarated with your own wife.
4. What does Proverbs 5:22-23 say to the man who will not be satisfied with his wife?

CHAPTER SEVENTEEN:

THE POWER OF GOD'S GRACE

Study Questions

1. Take a few moments to read and consider the opening story about "Jonadab." Explain in your own words what your initial feelings are about God's judicial system.

2. Write out the definition of patience given by the *Theological Dictionary of the N.T.*

3. Complete the sentence which begins, "It is extremely dangerous…"

4. After years of cultivating you spiritually, what is it that "He expects to one day" do?

5. What is it "easy to get carried away with?"

6. What is "the dangerous thing about savoring God's love while in a state of unrepentant sin?"

7. Did Jesus' love for "the rich young ruler" determine his eternal destiny or was it determined by "his response to that ardent love?" Explain your answer.

8. What is it that the author is "convinced" of concerning grace?

9. According to Dietrich Bonhœffer, why is "Such grace… *costly?*" (two sentences)

10. According to John MacArthur, what "is not a genuine salvation?"

11. Write out the quote from the "old-time Baptist preacher."

12. What are "those who imagine that they can remain in unrepentant sin" really saying?

13. What is "very important for the man whose life is characterized by lustful acts to know?"

What the Scriptures Say

1. Read the following verses and tell what you learn about sin.

Matthew 5:28-29

Galatians 5:19-21

I Corinthians 6:9-10

Hebrews 10:26-31

II Peter 2:20-21

I John 3:7-9

Read Luke 15:1-32 and answer the following questions.

What did the shepherd say in verse 6?

Write out what Jesus says about this in verse 7.

When the younger son finally came to an end of himself (in verse 19), how did the father respond in verse 20?

Personal Examination

1. What did you learn about God's grace from this chapter?

2. What did you learn about the way you have responded to that grace in the past from this chapter? What is your response now?

Group Discussion Questions

1. Read and discuss the fear of the Lord in the following verses: Proverbs 1:7; 3:7; 10:27; 14:26-27; 16:6; 19:23; 23:17; and Luke 12:5.

ANSWERS

Chapter One

1. a. careers, b. homes, c. personal attractiveness, d. other people, e. food, f. entertainment, g. sports, h. drugs. 2. a. exhibitionist, b. indecent phone caller, c. voyeur, or "peeping Tom", d. "john", e. chat room visitor, f. compulsive homosexual, g. child molester. 3. The indecent phone caller. 4. Their actual routines may differ but they all have a distinct or observable pattern which eventually led to their "acting out" sexually. 5. a. holding down a job, b. paying the bills. 6. Loved ones usually feel an inexplicable separation growing between the addict and themselves. 7. Having to come to grips with his addiction. 8. This blameshifting process might be taking place only in a sex addict's mind, as he seeks to justify his actions or shift responsibility toward those around him. 9. He lashes out at others with criticism. 10. The man who is being controlled by sin. 11. Another phenomenon the sexual addict faces is paranoia, imagining that others know about his secret behavior. 12. All socioeconomic, racial, and ethnic groups.

Chapter Two

1. The determination to fight for a pure life. 2. He will find ways to excuse, blameshift or otherwise justify continuing to live in his sin. 3. Just as the physical heart pumps life-giving blood throughout the entire physiological being, so too the inner heart of man functions as the nucleus of all that goes on in a person's life. 4. a. To set the heart upon, that is, long for..., b. Sinful longing; the inward sin which leads to the falling away from God, c. A longing for the unlawful, hence, concupiscence, desire, lust...the sensual desire connected with adultery, fornication. 5. a. The man's response may range from a quick glance to a longing, sinful gaze, b. The man purposely uses the faculties of his mind for immoral purposes--with or without outside influence. 6. a. They all love him, b. None refuse to be with him, c. The girl is always flawless, d. There are no obnoxious odors, e. There are no menstrual periods, f. There are no diseases, g. There is no lack of interest, h. She does not act rudely, i. She is not critical of him, j. She is not looking to take advantage of him, k. She is not looking to get his money, l. She will be willing to perform any desired sexual act, m. She exists solely to serve him. 7. A wall

of unbelief that had formed from years of cold formalism. 8. He said exactly what He meant to say and it is very dangerous to put oneself in the position of explaining away His words. 9. For instance, if we are talking about a godly man who "walks with the Lord," but then--in a moment of uncharacteristic weakness--succumbs to temptation and lusts or masturbates, but repents and gets back on track, that would rightly be termed *stumbling*. 10. For the man who regularly indulges in lust or masturbation. 11. While occasions do exist wherein believers remain needlessly old-fashioned regarding particular issues, for the most part it seems that Christendom has become enormously contaminated by the sexualized culture in which we live, following one step behind an increasing wave of decadence. 12. Those who purpose to fill their lives with the temporal gratifications of this world.

Chapter Three

1. a. Sin will take you further than you ever wanted to go, b. keep you longer than you ever wanted to stay, c. cost you more than you can ever pay. 2. a. Failure to reverence and give gratitude to God, b. the darkening heart, c. the suppression of truth, d. given over to the lusts of the heart, e. given over, f. the reprobate mind, g. filled with all unrighteousness. 3. an attitude of ungratefulness. 4. Once a person reaches this point, his life quickly begins to be governed almost exclusively by his sin. 5. a. his mind becomes more polluted, b. his heart more blackened, c. his perspectives more distorted. 6. a. *"I'm walking with God. I just have this one little problem."* b. *"I'm going through a difficult period of my life right now. I'll come out of it."* c. *"I've tried to quit. I've tried to follow the steps this book outlines. Nothing changes. I'm just as addicted as I have ever been."* 7. That a person is left to his own lusts with no possibility of satisfying them. 8. Things they have done that actually left them nauseous afterwards. 9. He will give people what they have shown they desire. 10. The person is allowed to have what he has shown he truly wants. 11. a. whatever fear he might still retain for God, b. the law, c. his personal safety, or d. the possible loss of loved ones.

Chapter Four

1. These stories represent a massive underworld that is currently thriving within the realm of American Christianity. 2. a. First, sexual sin is shameful to admit. b. Secondly, even though our society does not consider fornication or even adultery to be shameful, these sins are considered big "no-no's" in the evangelical movement. c. Another factor that contributes to a man keeping his sin covered is that it is fairly easy to live a double life of outward religion and secret sexual sin. 3. Your own answer. 4. This is an extremely private place, an inner sanctum--a holy of holies, so to speak. 5. Your own answer. 6. a. I suppose it begins on the playground where kids can be so cruel to one another. b. The fear is deepened during the awkward teenage years, c. and becomes embedded during adulthood. 7. In essence, they ignore the importance of the inward life and choose to concentrate on presenting the most favorable outward appearance. 8. That he has no sin. 9. God loves him too much to allow him to remain bound to his secret sin. 10. Your own answer. 11. Keeping himself hyped up in a false sense of security will only keep him buried under the burden of unconfessed sin, which in turn will further the delusion about his spirituality. 12. Your own answer. 13. Your own answer.

Chapter Five

1. The corrupt nature within us. 2. a. Sin kills peace; b. it kills hope; c. it kills usefulness; d. it kills the conscience; and, e. it kills the soul. 3. First there cometh into mind a bare thought of evil,

then a strong imagination thereof, afterwards delight, and evil motion, and then consent. And so little by little our wicked enemy getteth complete entrance, for that he is not resisted at the beginning. 4. Promised fulfillment. 5. The craftiness of the enemy. 6. A trigger is any event or emotion which evokes an inevitable response. 7. a. The actual temptation, b. the physical build-up, and c. opportunity. 8. Your own answer. 9. Because the person sees only the instant gratification. 10. Forgetfulness of God. 11. Your own answer. 12. Rationalization. 13. Your own words. 14. Your own answer. 15. Your own answer. 16. I had become so conditioned to giving in to temptation that I convinced myself I could not overcome it.

Chapter Six

1. Your own answer. 2. The *here and now.* 3. The truth is, before a person can ever hope to overcome habitual sin, he must first be willing to take responsibility for his *own* actions. 4. Understanding that you are in your present circumstances because of the choices *you* have made for yourself. 5. "I had to look elsewhere because my wife refuses to meet my needs." 6. It is this innate attraction for the forbidden that habitual sexual sin stems from. 7. That he be conformed into the image of His Son. 8. Denying self. 9. Pride is simply being filled with self and a sense of one's own importance. 10. a. a haughty spirit, b. self-protective pride, c. unapproachable pride, d. know-it-all pride, e. self-exalting pride, f. unsubmissive pride, and g. spiritual pride.

Chapter Seven

1. a. miracle, which occurs instantaneously, or b. through a process of change over an extended period of time. 2. Through a gradual, well-organized process of transforming the man into a new creation. 3. One of the things we must realize is that if God were to instantly set us free, it would then be much easier for us to return to old habits. 4. Your own answer. 5. God is often more concerned about exposing and expelling the underlying issues of the heart than He is about the outward sin with which the person struggles. 6. a. Will my selfishness simply be spent on being a workaholic? b. Will I live out the rest of my life with no concern for the lost who are going to hell around me? c. Will I continue to be self-centered with my family? d. Will those at work have to continually endure my temper? 7. A life transformed from one of corruption and utter uselessness to one of fruitfulness and purpose. 8. a. surmount, b. prevail against, c. subjugate, d. master, and e. overpower. 9. Your own answer. 10. a. Has the person been doing it for years? b. Has he been in denial over his problem? c. Has he been refusing to face responsibility for his actions? d. How deep has he gone into depravity? The answers to these questions are your own. 11. Your own answer.

Chapter Eight

1. Your own answer. 2. When we reach the point where we realize that our own efforts are getting us nowhere. 3. a. We get a certain amount of sympathy, b. it allows us to escape responsibilities and c. it provides a form of excitement. 4. If change isn't happening in our lives, we may need to admit that we really don't want it. 5. Your own answer. 6. Your own answer. 7. Persistence in prayer. 8. Your own answer. 9. Christ. 10. who He is. 11. "to believe, also to be persuaded of, and hence, to place confidence in, to trust, signifies, in this sense of the word, reliance upon, not mere credence." 12. The unbelief that it fosters. 13. Your own answer.

Chapter Nine

1. a. the flesh, b. the world, and c. the enemy. 2. God wants married couples, whom He has enjoined, to enjoy each other--thus, He made sex a pleasurable experience. 3. An alcoholic could go through his entire life without ever handling another drink, but a sex addict must learn to control his appetites. 4. a. comfort, b. pleasure, and c. the preservation of self. 5. A corrupted nature bent toward sin. 6. heart, soul, mind, spirit, inward parts. 7. Through the five senses (touch, taste, sight, hearing, and smelling. 8. Just as the flesh grows stronger when we feed it with sensuous living, our spirit grows stronger when it is nourished with the things of God. 9. a. If we practice (or sow) ungodliness then we will desire (or reap) ungodliness. b. By the same token, if we practice godliness then we will desire a greater godliness, and c. Feelings always follow behavior. 10. They want the change too soon. 11. Six weeks. (Three weeks to "feel comfortable," and three more weeks to "make the practice part of oneself.") 12. Our own fallen nature.

Chapter Ten

1. With such overwhelming exposure as this, why should anyone be surprised that a young teenager turns into a sex addict? 2. "The carnal world would have us believe that pleasure is the only purpose of sex. Some prudish Christians think that pleasure has nothing to do with sex. Both are wrong." 3. To *separate* ourselves from the world. 4. That is just not true. Satan is subtle—he develops attitudes slowly. 5. Your own answers. 6. Network television. 7. These words create an image of a soldier standing on guard duty, expecting to be attacked by enemy forces at any moment -- completely alert. 8. Rather than aggressively tearing down the strongholds of the enemy and waging war for the souls of our loved ones, we have allowed the enemy to ravage, plunder and exploit us. Instead of affecting the world around us for the cause of Christ, we have allowed this world's system to dictate our lives.

Chapter Eleven

1. Your own answer. 2. To the one who struggles with depression, a devil of dark gloom would be appointed. For those who battle a hot temper, a spirit of rage or murder would be given the task; and for an exaggerated sex drive, an unclean spirit would be commissioned. 3. Your own answer. 4. Your own answer. 5. That the person who *habitually* transgresses God's laws is in league with Satan -- the great rebel himself. 6. The result is always an increased degree of demon influence. 7. Your own answer. 8. Your own answer. 9. Those who have become accustomed to losing spiritual battles. 10. Your own answer.

Chapter Twelve

1. The common philosophy of dealing with addictions that the radio host, and countless others, advocate is that once a man is addicted to some vice, whether it is alcohol, drugs, gambling or sexual activity, he will *always* be addicted to it. 2. Your own answer. 3. God changes people from the inside out. 4. This change occurs as the person sees his need for change, comes to grip with his sinful behavior, and experiences a genuine turning away from that lifestyle. 5. A tremendous upheaval of his entire inner man is necessary. 6. For a person to believe that he can "repent" of some sin, without changing his way of thinking. 7. *Spiritual repentance is an experience whereby a person's will is altered for the express purpose of bringing it into line with God's will.*

8. Your own answer. 9. The transforming of a person from being one who does his own (carnal) will, to one who does the will of his Father. 10. Your own answer. 11. Your own answer. 12. Your own answer.

Chapter Thirteen

1. A man who does not heed instruction nor receive "the life-giving reproof." 2. Your own answer. 3. Your own answer. 4. Between the wise and the foolish. 5. That Peter would learn to discern the difference between the voice of the Holy Spirit and the voice of the enemy. 6. Sometimes a sharp rebuke is the very thing we need to get us back on track -- to bring us down off our "high horse," so to speak. 7. The words of a man who had been through the process of God's correction for over thirty years. 8. The person who will be loosed from sin must exhibit the character of someone who has indeed been set free. 9. Some sexual addicts see their sin as a minor quirk in an otherwise impeccable character. 10. "God can change a man in an instant, but it takes time to build character." 11. Holiness comes by the Lord's purging out of us our love for sin and for self.

Chapter Fourteen

1. He must learn to walk in the Spirit. 2. "IF... ye walk in the Spirit, THEN... ye shall not fulfill the lust of the flesh" 3. Jehovah Himself. 4. Lifestyle. 5. An ongoing condition of a person's life. 6. Your own answers. 7. One problem sexual addicts face is that their thinking has been warped through years of abuse and damage caused by their exposure to pornography and lewd fantasy. 8. A sincere repentance experienced. 9. A divine energy. 10. Getting God's Word on the inside to saturate our lives, thoughts, attitudes, emotions, and actions, so that we are conformed from the inside out into the likeness of Jesus Christ. 11. Regularly read the Scriptures, prayerfully do as they say, according to schedule, regardless of how you feel.

Chapter Fifteen

1. It will require some sacrificial severing to repair the damage. 2. Spiritual atmospheres conducive to lust. 3. In practical terms, the spirit of this world capitalizes upon the fact that humans have carnal desires which are innate within them: the lust for pleasure, the lust for gain, and the lust for position. 4. a. "...a mall...promotes covetousness," b. "...a boxing match...incites pride, anger and ultimately, violence," and c. "...a bar, the ambience puts him in a partying mood." 5. Must do everything within his power to minimize the enemy's ability to affect him spiritually. 6. Lustful living is hellish living. 7. Retraces his steps. 8. "I want! I want! I want!" 9. "Look at all I have! Thank You Lord, for all that You have done for me and given me. I don't need anything else." 10. Your own answer. 11. Gratitude is a disposition of the heart. 12. Your own answer. 13. A transformation will have to take place within. 14. To give of oneself. 15. Your own answer.

Chapter Sixteen

1. The reality of the self-centered gigolo who moves from woman to woman, desperately trying to fill an emptiness in his life. 2. Extremely shallow and goes no deeper than the emotions one is feeling at any particular time. 3. That commitment is only as secure as a person's fluctuating

passions. 4. This level of devotion to another person is not difficult for the man who is living his life with a sincere concern for the needs and feelings of other people, especially his wife and family. 5. One's behavior, rather than one's feelings. 6. The man who wishes to be a great lover according to biblical standards has the wherewithal to do so; not simply because it is a choice he can make, but because the Holy Spirit resides within him and will love others through him. 7. The walls she has constructed over time will eventually come down. 8. The love life between him and his wife can be reestablished. 9. "We must picture Hell as a state where everyone is perpetually concerned about his own dignity and advancement, where everyone has a grievance, and where everyone lives the deadly serious passions of envy, self-importance, and resentment." 10. Having a wife who can help them through the process of restoration. 11. The memory of the sexual encounters of the past. 12. *If a man will learn to love his wife, in spite of how he may feel inside, God will take away the appetite he has for other women and will give him in its place a desire for his wife.* 13. They have lived in the fast lane of sexual experiences for so long they can hardly handle the slow lane and doing the speed limit. 14. No one can maintain that level. 15. Your own answer.

Chapter Seventeen

1. Your own answer. 2. "The majestic God graciously restrains his righteous wrath, as in his saving work for Israel... . He does so in covenant faithfulness but also out of regard for human frailty... . Forbearance, of course, is not renunciation but postponement with a view to repentance." 3. It is extremely dangerous for an individual involved in habitual sin to assume that because he has not yet had his "day of reckoning" for his misconduct that there will be no forthcoming judgment to face. 4. Reap a fruitful harvest. 5. The feelings produced by that love and to corrupt it into something it is not meant to be. 6. A person can actually be deceived, thinking he is in true fellowship with the Lord. 7. Your own answer. 8. What many people today are accepting as grace is really nothing more than *the presumptuous license to sin.* 9. "Such grace is *costly* because it calls us to follow, and it is *grace* because it calls us to follow *Jesus Christ.* It is costly because it costs a man his life, and it is grace because it gives a man the only true life." 10. "Any 'salvation' that does not alter a lifestyle of sin and transform the heart of the sinner." 11. "That's like the unrepentant thief who went before the judge pleading not to be sent to prison. He had no intention of quitting the behavior that got him into his predicament. He only wanted to be spared a prison sentence." 12. *"I don't want to be cleansed; I just want to be forgiven."* 13. As much as he has indulged in sin, God has an even greater measure of grace to overcome that sin.

OTHER BOOKS AVAILABLE BY PURE LIFE MINISTRIES

WHEN HIS SECRET SIN BREAKS YOUR HEART

What can be more devastating for a wife than to discover her husband has a secret obsession with pornography and other women? Yet, this is what countless Christian wives face every day. Kathy Gallagher has been there; she understands the pain of rejection, the feelings of hopelessness and the questions that plague a hurting wife.

In this collection of letters, Kathy imparts heart-felt encouragement by providing the practical, biblical answers that helped her find healing in the midst of her most trying storm. The 30-day journal offers wives a place to prayerfully reflect and meditate upon Kathy's letters.

A BIBLICAL GUIDE TO COUNSELING THE SEXUAL ADDICT

A SERIOUS book for Christian Counselors
Christian men scoping pornography...
Adulterous eyes in the pulpit...
Casual sex among singles...
Now, more than ever, the Church needs godly people willing to passionately impart biblical truths to those drowning in the cesspool of sexual idolatry. Tackle the tough issues with this practical guide gleaned from 20 years of experience!

INTOXICATED WITH BABYLON

Intoxicated With Babylon is by far Steve Gallagher's best writing; its strength is his sobering deliverance of the unvarnished truth to a Church rife with sensuality and worldly compromise. In a time when evangelical Christians seem content to be lulled to sleep by the spirit of Antichrist, *Intoxicated With Babylon* sounds a clarion wake-up call in an effort to draw the Body of Christ back to the Cross and holy living. Those with itching ears will find no solace here, but sincere believers will experience deep repentance and a fresh encounter with the Living God.

OUT OF THE DEPTHS OF SEXUAL SIN

A Cop. A Big City. A Secret Obsession with Sex.
was an aggressive deputy on the Los Angeles Sheriff's Department... but he had a dark secret. Behind the arrogant exterior was a man obsessed with the triple-X-rated underworld. Could God really bring something good out of a life so ravaged by sin? This book is the riveting story of a man who courageously battled his way out of deep darkness to pioneer Pure Life Ministries—the first ministry in the world to help men find freedom from sexual addiction.

Not your typical *"sinner-gets-saved-and-lives-happily-ever-after"* book.

FOR MORE RESOURCES VISIT US ONLINE AT WWW.PURELIFEMINISTRIES.ORG

NEW! *From* ASHES *to* BEAUTY

SPIRITUAL TRUTHS FOR REBUILDING & REVITALIZING YOUR MARRIAGE

THERE IS HOPE FOR EVERY MARRIAGE...
Even in the aftermath of sexual sin.

Jeff Colón's marriage stands as a testimony of God's power to restore any marriage, even one that has been ravaged by sexual sin and drug addiction. Christian marriages are under attack as never before. Couples are suffering more than ever under the same despair that once gripped Jeff and his wife, Rose – Is there really hope for my marriage?

THE ANSWER IS A RESOUNDING YES! ...but the solution wasn't the typical fare found in Christian marriage books. Jeff and Rose had to go to the heart of the problem... they needed something more than outward alterations; they needed an inner transformation. Jeff's personal journey and his experience counseling men and couples qualifies him to share the biblical truths that will restore any marriage *From Ashes to Beauty!*

Includes A Study Guide For Each Chapter

THE WALK SERIES

WHETHER USED INDIVIDUALLY OR COLLECTIVELY, EACH OF THESE BIBLE STUDIES IS A GREAT TOOL FOR PERSONAL GROWTH OR GROUP DISCIPLESHIP.

THE WALK OF REPENTANCE

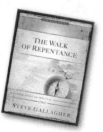

A 24-week Bible study for the Christian who desires to be more deeply consecrated to God. Experience the times of spiritual refreshing that follow repentance.

A LAMP UNTO MY FEET

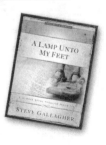

A 12-week journey through the beautiful Psalm 119 and the life of David. Every reader will be brought into a deeper love, respect and appreciation for God's Word.

PRESSING ON TOWARD THE HEAVENLY CALLING

The Prison Epistles are a divine archive of profound revelations about the kingdom of God. This 12-week study will challenge you to reach for the abundant life in God that Paul testifies is available to every one of us.

HE LEADS ME BESIDE STILL WATERS

A practical study of the choicest Psalms. This 12-week study takes you right into the intimate interactions between pious men and a loving, caring God and evokes a determined desire to find His Presence for yourself.

PURE LIFE MINISTRIES

Pure Life Ministries helps Christians achieve lasting freedom from sexual sin. The Apostle Paul said, "Walk in the Spirit and you will not fulfill the lust of the flesh." Since 1986, Pure Life Ministries (PLM) has been discipling men and women into the holiness and purity of heart that comes from a Spirit-controlled life. At the root, illicit sexual behavior is sin and must be treated with spiritual remedies. Our counseling programs and teaching materials are rooted in the biblical principles that, when applied to the believer's daily life, will lead him out of bondage and into freedom in Christ.

BIBLICAL TEACHING MATERIALS

Pure Life Ministries offers a full line of books, audio CDs and DVDs specifically designed to give men and women the tools they need to live in sexual purity.

RESIDENTIAL CARE

The most intense and involved counseling PLM offers comes through the **Live-In Program** (6-12 months), in Dry Ridge, Kentucky. The godly and sober atmosphere on our 45-acre campus provokes the hunger for God and deep repentance that destroys the hold of sin in men's lives.

HELP AT HOME

The **Overcomers At-Home Program** (OCAH) is available for those who cannot come to Kentucky for the Live-In program. This twelve-week counseling program features weekly counseling sessions and many of the same teachings offered in the Live-In Program.

• CARE FOR WIVES

Pure Life Ministries also offers help to wives of men in sexual sin. Our wives' counselors have suffered through the trials and storms of such a discovery and can offer a devastated wife a sympathetic ear and the biblical solutions that worked in their lives.

PURE LIFE MINISTRIES
14 School St. • Dry Ridge • KY • 41035
Office: 859.824.4444 • Orders: 888.293.8714
info@purelifeministries.org
www.purelifeministries.org